May the love and light of Jesus enter your heart
to show you the way to live now and forever.

To: _____

From: _____

On this Day: _____

LIGHT FOR THE WORLD
A Catholic Kid's Guide to Advent and Christmas

Written and Curated by Tom Wall

Illustrated by Martin Whitmore

Layout by Ron Tupper

Aquinas Ventures, LLC
Green Bay, Wisconsin 54305

Nihil Obstat
Reverend James P. Massart, D. Min., Ph.D.

Imprimatur
The Most Reverend David L. Ricken, DD, JCL
Bishop of Green Bay

Green Bay, Wisconsin   USA

September 1, 2015

The *Nihil Obstat* and *Imprimatur* are official declarations that a book is considered to be free of doctrinal or moral error.
It is not implied that those who have granted the *Nihil Obstat* or *Imprimatur*
agree with the contents, opinions, or statements expressed.

FIRST EDITION

OurCatholicFuture.com

ISBN: 978-0-9908950-3-9
Printed in China.

Dedicated to...

All those who walk in darkness, yet continue seeking the Light.

May Christ fill your heart with the light of His love
and show you the way to the life He created for you.

Each Advent, as we wait for Jesus to come into our lives on Christmas day,
He waits for us to come and receive Him in the Eucharist.

With Gratitude to...

Bishop Bob Morneau - a true pastor, teacher and friend... *in persona Christi.*
Many lives are brighter because of your love for Christ and His Church, thank you.

Adeste Fidelis!

O come, all ye faithful, joyful and triumphant!
O come ye, O come ye to Bethlehem;
Come and behold Him
Born the King of Angels:

O come, let us adore Him,
O come, let us adore Him,
O come, let us adore Him,
Christ the Lord.

— O Come, *All Ye Faithful*
English Translation by Fr. Frederick Oakeley

Why do you think people are so nice at Christmas time?

For many people, Christmas is the "most wonderful time of the year".
Almost everywhere we go, we can see and feel that people are in the spirit
of Christmas.

The spirit of Christmas brings out our best qualities...
love, kindness, patience, joy, and generosity.

During the Christmas season, we're more loving to our friends and family.
We treat each other with more patience and kindness, and we happily give
to those who are in need.

As we get ready for Christmas each year, we open our hearts
to the love Jesus brought into the world the day He was born.
When we allow Jesus to fill our hearts with His love,
it overflows and spreads to all of the people around us.

It's been over 2,000 years since Jesus came into the world.
When we remember and celebrate His birth every Christmas,
we still encounter the love He brought with Him on that joyous day.

Imagine how wonderful life would be
if we'd keep our heart open
to receiving and sharing His love throughout the year!

The Annunciation
Feast Day: March 25

THE ANNUNCIATION

Even though we celebrate Advent and Christmas during the month of December, the life of Jesus on Earth officially begins when He was conceived on the Solemnity of the Annunciation of the Lord, March 25th. This is the day the angel Gabriel visited Mary and told her that God had chosen her to be the mother of Jesus.

Did you know?
The Annunciation is exactly nine months before Christmas!

In the sixth month the angel Gabriel was sent by God to a town in Galilee called Nazareth,
to a virgin engaged to a man whose name was Joseph, of the house of David.
The virgin's name was Mary. And he came to her and said, "Greetings, favored one! The Lord is with you."

But she was much perplexed by his words and pondered what sort of greeting this might be.
The angel said to her, "Do not be afraid, Mary, for you have found favor with God.
And now, you will conceive in your womb and bear a son, and you will name him Jesus.
He will be great, and will be called the Son of the Most High,
and the Lord God will give to him the throne of his ancestor David.
He will reign over the house of Jacob forever, and of his kingdom there will be no end."

Then Mary said, "Here am I, the servant of the Lord; let it be with me according to your word."
Then the angel departed from her. *Luke 1:26-33, 38 (NRSV)*

When God called Mary to be Jesus' Mother, she trusted His will and said 'Yes'.
What is God calling you to do? Who is God calling you to be?
Will you trust Him and say 'Yes'?

"Look, the virgin shall conceive and bear a son, and they shall name him Emmanuel,"
which means, "God is with us." *Matthew 1:23 (NRSV)*

ADVENT AND CHRISTMAS: THE SEASONS OF LIGHT, LOVE, AND LIFE

ORDINARY
TIME ENDS

1ST SUNDAY
OF ADVENT

2ND SUNDAY
OF ADVENT

3RD SUNDAY
OF ADVENT

SEASON OF ADVENT

The season of Advent is the beginning of the Church's liturgical year.
Advent starts on the Sunday closest to November 30th and continues until December 24.

I am the light of the world.
Whoever follows me will never walk in darkness
but will have the light of life.

John 8:12 (NRSV)

4TH SUNDAY
OF ADVENT

CHRISTMAS

EPIPHANY

BAPTISM
OF THE LORD

ORDINARY
TIME BEGINS

SEASON OF CHRISTMAS

The season of Christmas begins on Christmas Eve
and continues into January until the Feast of the Baptism of the Lord.

THE SEASON OF ADVENT

Did you know?

The word Advent comes from the Latin words 'ad venire' and 'adventus', which mean 'coming' and 'arrival'.

Although Jesus is already present in our lives every day, Advent is the time of year that we truly focus on God's incarnation and how Jesus came to save the world. During the four weeks of Advent, we await and prepare our hearts and minds for Jesus' birth.

Nearly 2,000 years ago, John the Baptist prepared everyone who lived near the Jordan River for Jesus' coming.

In those days John the Baptist appeared in the wilderness of Judea, proclaiming, "Repent, for the kingdom of heaven has come near."

This is the one of whom the prophet Isaiah spoke when he said, "The voice of one crying out in the wilderness: 'Prepare the way of the Lord, make his paths straight.'"

Now John wore clothing of camel's hair with a leather belt around his waist, and his food was locusts and wild honey. Then the people of Jerusalem and all Judea were going out to him, and all the region along the Jordan, and they were baptized by him in the river Jordan, confessing their sins.

"I baptize you with water for repentance, but one who is more powerful than I is coming after me; I am not worthy to carry his sandals. He will baptize you with the Holy Spirit and fire." *Matthew 3: 1-6, 11 (NRSV)*

The Nativity of St. John the Baptist
Feast Day: June 24

TRADITIONS OF ADVENT AND CHRISTMAS

ADVENT WREATH

The Advent Wreath is typically made of evergreen branches and consists of four candles. It contains many symbols of the season of Advent and Christmas. On each of the four Sundays of Advent, we light a new candle to symbolize our anticipation for the Incarnation of our Lord, the light of this dark world.

The circular shape symbolizes that the eternal Kingdom of God has no beginning or end.

The three violet candles represent prayer, penance, fasting, and almsgiving; connecting the season of Advent to the season of Lent. The one rose candle represents our joy and hope for the birth of Jesus and is lit on Gaudete Sunday, the third Sunday of Advent. The word '*Gaudete'* means 'rejoice' in Latin and represents our joy that Christmas is getting closer.

LIGHTING THE ADVENT WREATH

1st Sunday: Light the middle violet candle.

2nd Sunday: Light two violet candles.

3rd Sunday: Light the first two violet candles and the rose candle.

4th Sunday: Light all four candles.

ADVENT CALENDAR

The tradition of Advent Calendars started in Germany approximately two hundred years ago.

We use an Advent Calendar to help us count down each day that remains until Jesus' birth. As we open each new day on the Advent Calendar, we continue to prepare and reflect on how we can keep Jesus at the center of our lives.

NATIVITY SCENE

The Nativity Scene, also known as a crèche, was first introduced in 1223 by St. Francis of Assisi in Italy on Christmas Eve as a live manger scene with real people and animals.

The tradition of having a Nativity scene in churches and homes continues to this day. All pieces of the Nativity set should be displayed when it is initially set up, except for one.

The final piece of the Nativity Scene is baby Jesus, and shouldn't be added until Christmas!

THE JESSE TREE

The Jesse Tree, named after the father of King David, helps us recall many of the prophecies from the Old Testament that lead us to the New Testament and the birth of Jesus. Each day during Advent, we add an ornament to the Jesse Tree that represents an important event and then read about it in the Bible.

OLD TESTAMENT EVENTS

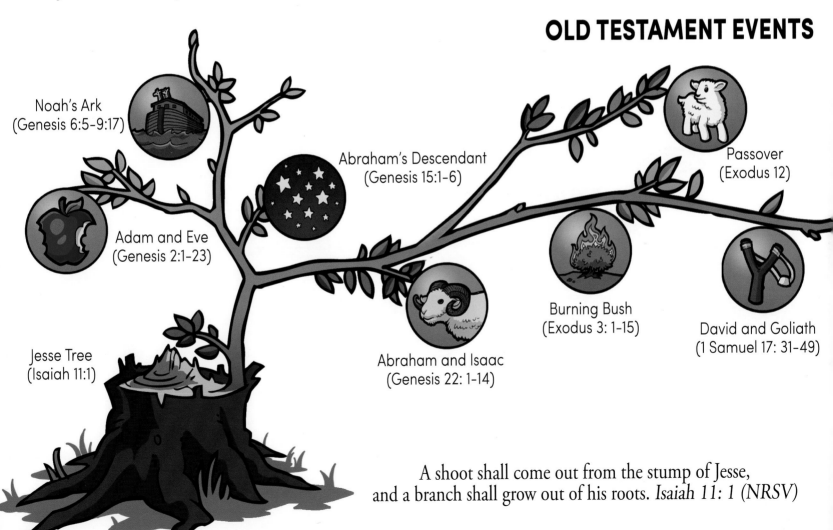

Noah's Ark
(Genesis 6:5-9:17)

Adam and Eve
(Genesis 2:1-23)

Abraham's Descendant
(Genesis 15:1-6)

Passover
(Exodus 12)

Burning Bush
(Exodus 3: 1-15)

David and Goliath
(1 Samuel 17: 31-49)

Abraham and Isaac
(Genesis 22: 1-14)

Jesse Tree
(Isaiah 11:1)

A shoot shall come out from the stump of Jesse, and a branch shall grow out of his roots. Isaiah 11: 1 (NRSV)

NEW TESTAMENT EVENTS

The Annunciation
(Luke 1:26-38)

His Name is John
(Luke 1:57-80)

The Three Magi
(Matthew 2:1-16)

John the Baptist
(Matthew 3)

Mary Visits Elizabeth
(Luke 1:39-56)

Joseph
(Matthew 1:18-25)

Jesus is Born
(Luke 2:8-20)

THE 'O' ANTIPHONS

The 'O' Antiphons are the short phrases that have been sung for over 1,300 years on the last seven days of Advent during Vespers (Evening Prayer). Each one comes from the Old Testament and tells of the coming of Jesus.

In the spirit of excitement and anticipation as we wait for Jesus' birth, all of these antiphons start with the joyous interjection 'O'. They also include another name we use to refer to God and contain the word 'Come'.

December 17: O **S**apientia (O Wisdom)

O Wisdom of our God Most High,
guiding creation with power and love:
come to teach us the path of knowledge!

December 18: O **A**donai (O Lord)

O Leader of the House of Israel,
giver of the Law to Moses on Sinai:
come to rescue us with your mighty power!

December 19: O **R**adix Jesse (O Root of Jesse)

O Root of Jesse's stem,
sign of God's love for all his people:
come to save us without delay!

December 20: O **C**lavis David (O Key of David)

O Key of David,
opening the gates of God's eternal Kingdom:
come and free the prisoners of darkness!

December 21: O **O**riens (O Dayspring)

O Radiant Dawn,
splendor of eternal light, sun of justice:
come and shine on those who dwell in darkness
and in the shadow of death.

December 22: O **R**ex Gentium (O King of the Nations)

O King of all nations and keystone of the Church:
come and save man, whom you formed from the dust!

December 23: O **E**mmanuel (O God With Us)

O Emmanuel, our King and Giver of Law:
come to save us, Lord our God!

- Lectionary for Mass for use in the United States of America

Did you know?

When the first letter from each of the seven Latin words is taken backwards, it spells **ERO CRAS**, which means... *"Tomorrow I will come!"*

FEAST DAYS DURING ADVENT

- **St. Francis Xavier** – December 3 (Memorial)

- **St. Nicholas** – December 6 (Optional Memorial)

- **St. Ambrose** – December 7 (Memorial)

- **Immaculate Conception (Holy Day of Obligation)** – December 8 (Solemnity)

- **St. Juan Diego** – December 9 (Optional Memorial)

- **Our Lady of Guadalupe** – December 12 (Feast)

- **St. Lucy** – December 13 (Memorial)

- **St. John of the Cross** – December 14 (Memorial)

ST. FRANCIS XAVIER
FEAST DAY: DECEMBER 3

St. Francis Xavier
1506-1552

"It is not the actual physical exertion that counts towards one's progress, nor the nature of the task, but by the spirit of faith with which it is undertaken."

St. Francis Xavier was a Spanish priest who was ordained in 1537.
He co-founded the Society of Jesus (Jesuits) with St. Ignatius of Loyola in 1540.

St. Francis Xavier devoted most of his priesthood to doing foreign mission work, evangelizing and spreading Christianity throughout Asian countries such as India, Japan, Malaysia, and Indonesia. Along with St. Thérèse of Lisieux, St. Francis Xavier is the co-patron saint of all Missionaries.

St. Francis Xavier was canonized by Pope Gregory XV in 1622.

ST. NICHOLAS

St. Nicholas was a Greek Bishop who lived in Myra, a city located on the Mediterranean coast in the country we now call Turkey. His faith was very strong as a child and he eventually decided to use the wealth he inherited from his parents to help the people in his region. Bishop Nicholas became well-known for his generosity with the poor, his kindness toward children, and his concern for sailors.

Stewardship Prayer

Generous and loving God,
You call us to be disciples of your Son Jesus
and good stewards of all your many gifts.
Open our minds and hearts to a greater awareness
and deeper appreciation
of your countless blessings.
Transform us through the power of your Spirit
to nurture a Stewardship way of life
marked by faith-filled prayer,
service to our neighbor
and generous sharing.
Teach us to be faithful servants of your gifts.
With Mary's help, may we return ten-fold
the gifts entrusted to us.
We pray through Christ, our Lord. Amen.

– Catholic Diocese of Green Bay

Prayer for Children

Lord, we thank you for all the children in our life.
Help us to teach them Your truth,
show them Your love,
and guide them along Your way;
so they may come to know You, love You, and serve You.
Continue to protect these precious gifts of ours
today and always. Amen.

– Tom Wall

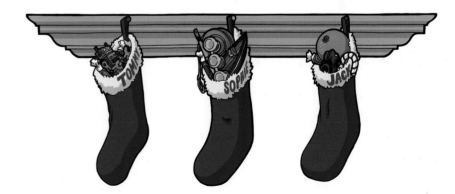

St. Nicholas started the tradition of filling kids' socks with gifts, and it continues today. We celebrate St. Nicholas Day on the anniversary of his death, December 6th.

THE IMMACULATE CONCEPTION

The Solemnity of the Immaculate Conception, a Holy Day of Obligation, is celebrated on December 8.

The Immaculate Conception, often confused with the Virgin Birth of Jesus to Mary, actually celebrates the conception of Mary to St. Joachim and St. Anne.

Parent's Prayer

All praise to you, Lord Jesus, Lover of children:
Bless our family and help us to lead our children to You.

Give us light, strength, and courage when our task is difficult
Let your spirit fill us with love and peace,
So that we may help our children to love you.

All glory and praise are yours, Lord Jesus, for ever and ever. Amen.

OUR LADY OF LOURDES

In 1856, the Virgin Mary appeared to a young French girl named Bernadette Soubirous a total of eighteen times on the mountainside of Lourdes, France. When Bernadette told the people of her town that a beautiful woman dressed in white and blue appeared to her, many of them didn't believe her. On each of these apparitions, Bernadette asked the woman who she was, but it wasn't until the seventeenth time that she told her...

"I am the Immaculate Conception".

St. Bernadette was canonized by Pope Pius XI on December 8, 1933, the Feast of the Immaculate Conception.

The Immaculate Conception
Feast Day: December 8
(Holy Day of Obligation)

St. Bernadette & Our Lady of Lourdes
Feast Day: April 16   Feast Day: February 11

St. Joachim & St. Anne
Feast Day: July 26

OUR LADY OF GUADALUPE

Our Lady of Guadalupe, the Patroness of the Americas, first appeared to Juan Diego on a hill near Mexico City on December 9, 1531. She told him she was the Mother of God and asked that a church be built on the site where she appeared to him.

When Juan Diego told the archbishop of Mexico City what happened, Archbishop Zumárraga sent him back to Tepeyac Hill to ask her for a sign. To prove her identity, Our Lady of Guadalupe cured Juan's uncle and also told him to pick a bunch of flowers and bring them back to the archbishop. Juan Diego went to the top of the hill and found colorful roses that didn't even grow in Mexico, especially in December!

He placed the flowers in his tilma and went back in to town on December 12. When Juan opened it, the rare roses fell to the floor in front of the archbishop and revealed the miraculous image of Our Lady of Guadalupe on the fabric of his tilma.

Juan Diego's tilma with the image of Guadalupe can be seen at the Basilica of Our Lady of Guadalupe in Mexico City, Mexico.

Prayer to the Virgin of Guadalupe

Hail, Mother of the Americas, Heavenly Missionary of the New World!
From the Sanctuary of Tepeyac you have been for more than four centuries
the Mother and Teacher of the Faith to the peoples of the Americas.
Be also our protection and save us, O Immaculate Mary.
Aid our rulers; stir up a new zeal in our prelates;
increase the virtues of our clergy; and preserve forever our Faith.
In every home may the holiness of the family flourish,
and in the shelter of the home may Catholic education, favored by your own benign glance,
achieve a wholesome growth.

— Pope St. John XXIII

ST. JOHN OF THE CROSS
FEAST DAY: DECEMBER 14

*"In the evening of life,
we will be judged on love alone."*

St. John of the Cross, O.C.D. was a Spanish priest, poet, and a mystic.
He studied and wrote about the relationship between God and our soul.
He wrote the majority of his most famous poem, called *The Spiritual Canticle*,
from a prison cell.

In addition to being a brilliant poet, St. John of the Cross reformed
the Carmelite Order when he co-founded the Discalced Carmelite Order
with St. Teresa of Avila in 1568. While a Carmelite Friar, he travelled
from town to town helping Carmelite nuns and friars open
Carmelite monasteries all over Spain.

St. John of the Cross, O.C.D. was canonized by Pope Benedict XIII in 1726.
He was declared one of only thirty-three Doctors of the Catholic Church
in 1926 by Pope Pius XI because of his important contribution to theology.

St. John of the Cross, O.C.D.
1542-1591

FEAST DAYS DURING CHRISTMAS

- **Christmas** (Holy Day of Obligation) – December 25 (Solemnity)

- **St. Stephen** – December 26 (Feast)

- **St. John, Apostle and Evangelist** – December 27 (Feast)

- **Holy Innocents** – December 28 (Feast)

- **Holy Family of Jesus, Mary, and Joseph** – First Sunday after Christmas (Feast)

- **Mary, the Holy Mother Of God** (Holy Day of Obligation) – January 1 (Solemnity)

- **St. Basil the Great & St. Gregory Nazianzen** – January 2 (Memorial)

- **St. Elizabeth Ann Seton** – January 4 (Memorial)

- **St. John Neumann** – January 5 (Memorial)

- **Epiphany** – Sunday between January 2 and January 8 (Solemnity)

- **Baptism of the Lord** – Sunday after the Epiphany (Feast)

CHRISTMAS (THE NATIVITY OF THE LORD)

After waiting and preparing our hearts and minds for the coming of our Lord during Advent, the day is finally here and it's time to rejoice! We celebrate the birth of Jesus on December 25, the Solemnity of the Nativity of the Lord.

At the beginning of Mass on Christmas Eve, it is customary to begin with the formal announcement of Jesus' birth, called *The Nativity of our Lord Jesus Christ*. It starts with the creation of the world and recalls events from the Old Testament until the birth of our Lord.

The Nativity of Our Lord Jesus Christ

The Twenty-fifth Day of December,

when ages beyond number had run their course
from the creation of the world,

when God in the beginning created heaven and earth,
and formed man in his own likeness;

when century upon century had passed
since the Almighty set his bow in the clouds after the Great Flood,
as a sign of covenant and peace;

in the twenty-first century since Abraham, our father in faith,
came out of Ur of the Chaldees;

in the thirteenth century since the People of Israel were led by
Moses in the Exodus from Egypt;

around the thousandth year since David was anointed King;

in the sixty-fifth week of the prophecy of Daniel;

in the one hundred and ninety-fourth Olympiad;

in the year seven hundred and fifty-two
since the foundation of the City of Rome;

in the forty-second year of the reign of Caesar Octavian Augustus,
the whole world being at peace,

JESUS CHRIST, eternal God and Son of the eternal Father,
desiring to consecrate the world by his most loving presence,
was conceived by the Holy Spirit,
and when nine months had passed since his conception,
was born of the Virgin Mary in Bethlehem of Judah,
and was made man:

The Nativity of Our Lord Jesus Christ according to the flesh.

- The Roman Martyrology

The real reason for the season of Christmas is to celebrate the birthday of our Lord Jesus Christ.

From the beginning of time, all of the prophets from the Old Testament spoke of this amazing day.
Every Christmas, we celebrate the Incarnation of Christ, the day God came from Heaven to Earth
to be among us and show us how to live and love.

Although Jesus was born in a manger to a family with very few possessions, He changed the world.
On December 25, Jesus came to bring God's light and love, and show us the way to His Father's Kingdom.

Each Christmas we welcome Him into our hearts so that He may enter and change our lives.

*For God so loved the world that he gave his only Son,
so that everyone who believes in him may not perish but may have eternal life.*
— John 3:16 (NRSV)

Did you know?

The word Christmas is an Old English word that combines the words 'Christ' and 'Mass'
and is approximately a thousand years old.

CHRIST + MASS = CHRISTMAS

In this one word, we are reminded of the two central parts of our Catholic faith.

We focus on the life of Jesus Christ and the Mass where He gave Himself to us through the Eucharist.
The reason it's so important we go to Mass is to encounter Jesus in the Scriptures,
in the Sacrament of the Eucharist, and in the community.

ST. JOHN, APOSTLE AND EVANGELIST

On December 27, we celebrate the Feast of St. John the Apostle and Evangelist. St. John the Evangelist, known as the Apostle of Love, was one of Jesus' closest friends. He and his brother James were fishermen when Jesus invited them to put down their nets and follow Him. Along with being one of the Twelve Apostles, St. John is also credited with writing the Gospel of John, the three Epistles of John, and the Book of Revelation.

Beloved, let us love one another, because love is from God;
everyone who loves is born of God and knows God.
Whoever does not love does not know God, for God is love.
God's love was revealed among us in this way:
God sent his only Son into the world so that we might live through him.
In this is love, not that we loved God but that he loved us
and sent his Son to be the atoning sacrifice for our sins. *1 John 4:7-10 (NRSV)*

GOD → JESUS → US → OTHERS

| God is love. | Jesus came to Earth to share His love, and save the world. | We were born to receive His love. | We are called to share His love with one another. |

St. John the Apostle and Evangelist
Feast Day: December 27

The Holy Innocents
Feast Day: December 28

THE HOLY INNOCENTS

On December 28, we remember the Feast of the Holy Innocents. This feast day recalls when King Herod heard about a baby who was just born in Bethlehem and would someday become king. Out of fear that King Herod would be overthrown by the new King, he became very angry. He sent his soldiers out to find and kill all baby boys under the age of two so none of them could overtake his throne.

Now after they had left, an angel of the Lord appeared to Joseph in a dream and said, "Get up, take the child and his mother, and flee to Egypt, and remain there until I tell you; for Herod is about to search for the child, to destroy him." Then Joseph got up, took the child and his mother by night, and went to Egypt, and remained there until the death of Herod. This was to fulfill what had been spoken by the Lord through the prophet, "Out of Egypt I have called my son."

When Herod saw that he had been tricked by the wise men, he was infuriated, and he sent and killed all the children in and around Bethlehem who were two years old or under, according to the time that he had learned from the wise men. *Matthew 2:13-16 (NRSV)*

Prayer for the Dignity of Human Life

Lord and giver of all life,
help us to value each person,
created in love by you.

In your mercy, guide and assist our efforts
to promote the dignity and value of all human life,
born and unborn.

We ask this through Christ our Lord. Amen.

THE HOLY FAMILY OF JESUS, MARY, AND JOSEPH

We celebrate the Feast of the Holy Family on the first Sunday after Christmas in honor of Jesus, Mary, and Joseph. On this special Sunday, we pray for families throughout the world and remember how important they are to the past, present, and future of the Catholic Church.

Prayer for Families

We bless your name, O Lord,
for sending your own incarnate Son,
to become part of a family,
so that, as he lived its life,
he would experience its worries and its joys.

We ask you, Lord,
to protect and watch over this family,
so that in the strength of your grace
its members may enjoy prosperity,
possess the priceless gift of your peace,
and, as the Church alive in the home,
bear witness in this world to your glory.

We ask this thought Christ our Lord. Amen.

- Book of Blessings

St. Joseph, Protector of the Holy Family, Pray for All Families Around the World.

The Holy Family
Feast Day: First Sunday after Christmas

Solemnity of Mary, the Holy Mother of God
Feast Day: January 1
(Holy Day of Obligation)

Our Lady
of Perpetual Help
Feast Day: June 27

SOLEMNITY OF MARY, THE HOLY MOTHER OF GOD

In addition to being New Year's Day, the first day of January is also an important feast day. On January 1, we celebrate the Feast of the Solemnity of Mary, the Holy Mother of God. On this is Holy Day of Obligation, we honor Mary for being the Mother of Jesus.

Hail, Holy Queen
(The Salve Regina)

Hail, Holy Queen, Mother of Mercy,
our life, our sweetness, and our hope!
To you do we cry, poor banished children of Eve;
To you do we send up our sighs,
mourning and weeping in this vale of tears.
Turn, then, most gracious advocate,
your eyes of mercy toward us;
and after this our exile,
show unto us the blessed fruit of your womb, Jesus.
O clement, O loving, O sweet Virgin Mary!

Pray for us, O holy Mother of God,
that we may be made worthy of the promises of Christ.

Prayer for Mothers

Loving God,
as mother gives life and nourishment to her children,
so you watch over your Church.
Bless our mother.

Let the example of her faith and love shine forth.
Grant that we, her family,
may honor her always
with a spirit of profound respect
Grant this through Christ our Lord. Amen.

- Catholic Household Blessings and Prayers

OUR LADY OF PERPETUAL HELP

The icon of *Our Lady of Perpetual Help*, also known as Our Mother of Perpetual Help, is a piece of Byzantine art that was created in the 15th century. This famous icon of Mary is located in Rome, Italy at the Church of St. Alphonsus Liguori and is cared for by the Redemptorist priests.

ST. ELIZABETH ANN SETON

FEAST DAY: JANUARY 4

*"We must pray without ceasing,
in every occurrence and employment of our lives -
that prayer which is rather a habit of lifting up the heart
to God as in a constant communication with Him."*

St. Elizabeth Ann Seton, S.C., the first saint born in the United States, devoted her life to educating and caring for children.

She lived in New York City with her husband, their five children, and her husband's seven younger siblings after their dad passed away. After her husband got sick and died, St. Elizabeth Ann Seton converted to Catholicism and worked hard to raise and educate all of the kids left under her care.

She eventually moved to Maryland and opened the nation's first Catholic school, laying the foundation for the Catholic parochial school system in the United States. She also founded the Sisters of Charity, the first community of religious sisters in the United States, and became known as Mother Seton.

St. Elizabeth Ann Seton, S.C. was canonized by Pope Paul VI in 1975.

St. Elizabeth Ann Seton, S.C.
1506-1552

ST. JOHN NEUMANN

FEAST DAY: JANUARY 5

"Lord, teach me how to live."

St. John Neumann, C.Ss.R., the fourth bishop of the Diocese of Philadelphia, was the first American bishop to be declared a saint.

Originally from Bohemia, St. John Neumann learned six languages before coming to the United States in 1836 to be ordained a priest and live in New York. A few years later he became a Redemptorist priest and moved to Maryland. In 1852 he was appointed bishop of the Diocese of Philadelphia, now an Archdiocese. Because he spoke so many languages, he served various immigrant communities throughout Philadelphia.

While he was bishop, St. John Neumann created and organized the first diocesan Catholic school system.

St. John Neumann, C.Ss.R. was canonized by Pope Paul VI in 1977.

St. John Neumann, C.Ss.R.
1811-1860

The Epiphany
Feast Day: Sunday between January 2 and January 8

THE EPIPHANY

We celebrate the Epiphany of the Lord, the day the Son of Man was made manifest to the Magi, on the Sunday between January 2 and January 8. This is the day the three Magi traveled to meet and honor our newborn Savior with gifts of gold, frankincense, and myrrh.

Did you know?

The Christmas tradition of giving and receiving gifts started when the three Wise Men brought gifts to the baby Jesus. In many countries around the world, kids receive their Christmas presents on January 6, the day of the Epiphany of the Lord.

PRESENTS OR PRESENCE?

During Christmas it's easy to get distracted by all of the gifts and celebrations. Although it's fun to give and receive Christmas gifts, the most important gift we can receive and give is Jesus. We need to remember that the Lord's presence in our life is more important than the presents around the Christmas tree.

Just like the three Wise Men, we need to focus on the Lord, and give generously and spread the Good News!

Rosca de Reyes
(Kings' Cake)

The *Rosca de Reyes*, is a tradition in many Spanish-speaking countries.

Hidden inside the cake is a small doll of the baby Jesus, representing when the Holy Family fled to Egypt to hide Jesus from Herod.

THE BAPTISM OF THE LORD

On the Sunday after the Solemnity of the Epiphany, we celebrate when Jesus was baptized by John the Baptist in the Jordan River. Christmas Time closes with the Feast of the Baptism of the Lord.

Then Jesus came from Galilee to John at the Jordan, to be baptized by him.
John would have prevented him, saying, 'I need to be baptized by you, and do you come to me?'
But Jesus answered him, 'Let it be so now; for it is proper for us in this way
to fulfill all righteousness.' Then he consented. And when Jesus had been baptized,
just as he came up from the water, suddenly the heavens were opened to him
and he saw the Spirit of God descending like a dove and alighting on him.
And a voice from heaven said, 'This is my Son, the Beloved, with whom I am well pleased.'

Matthew 3:13-17 (NRSV)

The Baptism of the Lord
Feast Day: Sunday after the Epiphany

Over 2,000 years ago God sent His only Son to be the Light of the world.

Jesus was born to teach us how to love and how to live,
and invited His disciples to follow Him.

How will people know that you are one of His disciples?

They will know that you are one of His followers because of how you live.
They will see Jesus in you by the way you treat other people.
They will come to know Him, through you.

We are called to love and to live like Jesus did. We are called to imitate Him.

Every Christmas, Jesus is born in your heart
so that you may share His love, light, and life
with the people you encounter every day.

Thanks be to God for his indescribable gift!

2 Corinthians 9:15 (NRSV)

Silent Night

Silent night, holy night,
all is calm, all is bright
round yon virgin mother and child.
Holy infant, so tender and mild,
sleep in heavenly peace,
sleep in heavenly peace.

Silent night, holy night,
shepherds quake at the sight;
glories stream from heaven afar,
heavenly hosts sing Alleluia!
Christ the Savior is born,
Christ the Savior is born!

Silent night, holy night,
Son of God, love's pure light;
radiant beams from thy holy face
with the dawn of redeeming grace,
Jesus, Lord, at thy birth,
Jesus, Lord, at thy birth.

Silent night, holy night,
wondrous star, lend thy light;
with the angels let us sing,
Alleluia to our King;
Christ the Savior is born,
Christ the Savior is born!

Lyrics Written by Fr. Joseph Mohr
Music Composed by Franz Xaver Gruber